2 Selling at Exhibitions – Robert Jakobsen

This page is intentionally left blank

Selling at Exhibitions

Exhibitor's Handbook

Robert M. Jakobsen
Selling at Exhibitions
© Robert M. Jakobsen – info@salgskurser.info
ISBN-13: 978-1482609028
ISBN-10: 1482609029
First published by © Robert M. Jakobsen 2009

Translated into English and revised by Peter Clarke & Helgi Eidesgaard © 2013

Introduction

Exhibitions, Fairs or Shows exist to offer an ideal marketing platform for selling both products and services. For the visitors, they offer a meeting place where potential buyers with similar interests can compare solutions from different vendors and catch up on the latest developments within their field of expertise or interest. For the exhibitors, they offer the chance to showcase their products or capabilities, to announce new products and services, to meet new prospective clients and to catch up with existing clients.

There are several types of exhibitions:

Trade Shows target a particular profession. These include shows like the Drives and Controls Exhibition in Birmingham, specialising in equipment for industrial automation and similar specialist events. These are business to business events.

Closed Trade Shows only allow access to a certain type of visitor and are not open to the general public. The visitors can, for example, be invited guests from the target industry or potential purchasers from that industry.

Public Exhibitions are open to the general public. The best example would probably be the Ideal Home Show which features a wide range of products for the home. Smaller ones may be held to promote specific consumer goods with a well-defined audience. This could be holidays, wedding planning, food, or much more. These are business to consumer events.

Companies often spend a lot of time and money on planning and executing exhibitions, so it is important to maximise the returns on the investment.

Unfortunately, all too often there are examples of employees on the exhibition stands who do not have the desired body language and the necessary enthusiasm.

One of the major errors many companies make is the lack of follow-up after the show. This book gives advice on the planning and execution of exhibitions, along with tips and tricks about the process, from start to finish.

About the Author:

Robert Jakobsen is founder of Salgskurser.info and magicofsales.com.
Robert teaches sales techniques and methodologies, including selling at shows, negotiating techniques, presentation techniques and the use of Neurolinguistic programming (NLP) in sales. Robert is the author of the book *NLP in selling* (in English) as well as co-author of a Danish textbook of sales.

Chapter 1: Marketing

Before you decide on the appropriate marketing mix it is important to identify your goal(s) for the exhibition:

- Introduce a new product or service
- Strengthen your corporate image
- Meet new prospects
- Generate leads
- Take orders
- Obtain email addresses
- Identify distributors, resellers or other partners
- Make appointments for meetings, presentations or demonstrations
- Make an impact!

When setting goals for the exhibition, it is a good idea to use **smarter** goals:

- **S**pecific
- **M**easurable
- **A**ttainable
- **R**ealistic
- **T**ime-bound
- **E**valuate
- **R**e-evaluate

Specific
Your objective should be very precise and well-defined.
Measurable
You need to be able to identify when you have reached your goal. You need to monitor your activities to ensure you are being successful in reaching your objectives.
Attainable
The goal must be important, relevant and reasonable. It must also be acceptable to all members of the team involved with the show.
Realistic
You must believe that the objective can be achieved. Be ambitious but realistic.
Time-bound
How long will you work towards the goal? How much time will you allocate towards achieving this goal?
Evaluate
When and how will you evaluate and refine the goal?
Re-evaluate
Re-evaluate your goals to make sure you are on the right track, and do that as often as necessary. Make sure to keep your ultimate outcome in mind, and ask yourself what your purpose is, and what is your action plan to reach your ultimate result / goal?

Other things to consider are:

- What is your target audience?
- Where do you get your existing customers from?
- Do you want your distributors, resellers or partners to participate with you in the show?
- Can you recover any of your costs? If you are selling on behalf of a supplier they may be willing to contribute to the cost of the exhibition. If you are sharing your space with a distributor or partner they may also be willing to make a contribution.
- Are you certain the show is relevant to your business?
- What other shows are relevant?
- Who are the decision makers and will they be at the show?

To make sure you have prepared for the show, fill in the following information and bring the list to the exhibition:

Our target audience is:

_____

_____

_____

_____

_____

Our sales message is:

_____

_____

_____

_____

_____

_____

Our USP's (Unique Selling Points/Propositions) are:

_____

_____

_____

_____

_____

_____

_____

_____

_____

USP: **What are Your Unique Selling Points / Propositions?**

The concept was created by Rosser Reeves from Ted Bates & Company in 1940.

Each proposition must present a unique benefit for the customer – not just words, "hot air", or "window dressing". Each proposition must say: "Buy this product, and you will get this specific result/benefit."

The proposition must be one that the competition does not, or cannot, offer. It must be unique — either a uniqueness of the brand or a claim not otherwise made in that particular field of advertising.

Your USP is what makes you and your product or service unique.

"Why should I buy from you?" The problem most people have when they plan their marketing strategy is that they answer the first part of this question - **"why should I buy?"** - But not the second part - **"from you?"** You need to differentiate yourself from your competitors.

Identify your USP. All kinds of marketing strategy are really flawed without this.

Marketing for an Exhibition

Implementing marketing initiatives before a trade show can have a significant impact on how much of a success the show will be.

The most effective action is probably by distributing personal invitations. These may be delivered in person or over the telephone, followed by a ticket, a letter or an email invitation.

Telemarketing aimed at prospective target customers for your products is very effective. This can be done by your own salespeople or outsourced to an external telemarketing company.

A script for inviting potential customers to the show over the telephone could sound something like this:

"Hello. This is (your name) _____ calling from (Company Name) _____. I am calling to invite you to the (name of show) _____ which is being held at (venue) _____ from (dates) _____.

Have you visited this exhibition in the past?

Would you like me to send you tickets for the show?"

Here you can possibly discuss some of the topics which may be of interest and follow up, where appropriate, with a remark that it is always nice to follow the latest trends in the industry.

If the prospect accepted tickets to the show, you should now aim to set-up up a time for an appointment at the show.

If the prospect declines tickets as he / she is unable to find time to attend, then you should take this opportunity to try to set up a direct meeting with him / her.

You can, for example, say: "It is unfortunate that you are unable to visit the show since we have a lot of exciting new announcements. Since I have you on the phone, could we perhaps arrange a suitable time for a meeting so I can update you after the show?" *Then propose some possible dates.*

Alternatively: "It is unfortunate that you will not be able to visit the show. Do you perhaps have any colleagues that might be interested and are available to attend?"

Direct-Mail

Direct-mail to relevant customers and prospects can, if done correctly, be very effective. In some cases, it is a good idea to build a campaign with 2-3 letters with different content. These could include a preview of new products being launched, a ticket and a count-down to the show. A good incentive can be a gift you are offering attendees of the show or entrance to a competition with an interesting gift.

The internet is also a good place to run campaigns for the exhibition. Landing pages (the page reached by clicking on your ad) are important for this. Search engine optimisation on Google AdWords is quick to produce, and a landing page promoting the show can provide extra visitors to your stand at the show at a manageable cost.

A business blog about your trade show participation can also be a very good idea.

The landing page should be carefully prepared to make it easy to use, whether it be information about purchasing your products, downloading your brochures, signing up for your newsletter or completing a questionnaire. The keywords that are used must be relevant to ensure the effectiveness of your campaign.

Promotional Gifts

Promotional gifts can offer an effective way of marketing at shows. However, you need to be original and make sure that you stand out and are remembered. If possible, try to have personalised gifts with the visitor's name and your logo. This, of course, is only practical when you have the names of the invited guests beforehand. However, it will get you remembered, so it is worth it. The other option is to send out the gifts (if economically viable) after the show when you have collected the names you need.

Make sure that the gift has a perceived value: it should not be seen as "cheap" and, ideally, should have a practical purpose so that it is used and remembered.

A good way to increase the value of the gift is to use Dr. Robert B. Cialdini's so-called 'Scarcity Principle'. In his book, *Influence: The Psychology of Persuasion*, scarcity is a strong motivating factor that can be exploited by promotional gifts. This could, for example, be various lines of clothing of limited quantity, or other gift items where the quantity in circulation is limited.

This principle can also be used in general sales technique, being particularly effective when closing the sale.

Cialdini also describes the reason: *The Rule for Reciprocation* is good with promotional gifts and gifts in general, where you are looking to get something in return for what you have given.

When we receive a gift, we feel indebted to the person who gives us the gift. This rule is so strong that it can overcome our feelings of hostility or suspicion towards the person who gives us the gift.

Marcel Mauss notes in his study of gift-giving that there is an obligation to provide, an obligation to receive and an obligation to repay.

It is this series of interconnected obligations which can be utilised, and although the obligation to repay is the key of the repayment rule, it is the obligation to receive that makes the rule so easy to exploit.

To make a gift look attractive, it is always a good idea to use branded products, because then the gift – and its promotional value – will last longer. You must be careful to make sure that the gift suits the target audience.
Remember, too, that the gift, if suitable for the workplace, will also be seen by colleagues and visitors, thus increasing the marketing value.
Alternatively, it can be a good idea to think of things that will appeal to children, the family or something else that is practical for the home.

Things to consider before the promotional gifts are chosen:

- What is your budget?
- What do you want to achieve?
- Who should have what and why?
- What is the message you want to put across?
- How will you inform your audience?
- How will you measure the results?

Here is a list of 10 of the most popular promotional gifts:

1. Ball point pens
2. Neck straps / lanyards
3. Water bottles
4. Bags
5. Caps

6. Key rings with attached shopping cart coin / token
7. Reflectors
8. Small stuffed animals
9. Footballs
10. Brainteasers

Promotion through newspapers, trade press, radio, television and on billboards, buses and other local channels is also useful.

The trade press is very important as it reaches an audience with a specific interest in your products. Lists of trade magazines for your area of business can easily be found using your favourite search engine. If, for example, you were interested in industry (electronics, process control, instrumentation, energy management, factory equipment) then this publisher can offer a selection of titles - www.**connectingindustry**.com.

www.**allyoucanread**.com is another very useful place where you, among a host of other things, can find local magazines etc.

Newsletters are also an effective marketing tool.

Press releases may also have a good effect. You should either keep an up-to-date list of the trade magazines relevant to your business, along with their editor's details, or work with a PR-agency that specialises in your area of business.

Use PR at Exhibitions
It is essential for a new company to get a positive mention

in the right magazines. It allows you to gain exposure in the "right place" without requiring a massive advertising budget. The focused trade press is more likely to include your material, since it has a high probability of being relevant to their audience. You are much less likely to get exposure in the general media unless you have a product with a very wide audience.

Aim for Impact

Putting aside the prestige of being mentioned in the main daily newspapers, there are good opportunities in the local press and, of course, the specialised trade press. Whilst the major national daily newspapers reach millions of people, you will often find that the majority are not your target audience (unless, of course, you are selling a mass consumer product). Furthermore, they tend to have a short lifespan – as they used to say: "Today's news is tomorrow's fish and chip wrapper". To get your message in the national press you will undoubtedly pay a high price and still not be able to put across a strong message. The specialised trade press will, of course, have a much smaller circulation and range, but its readers are more likely to be interested in your business. The costs are also less inhibitive and will allow you much more scope for being creative and presenting a strong image or message. This gives you the opportunity to get the right message across to the right audience.

Online Media

In recent years, online media has grown dramatically and continues to do so. Large numbers of niche websites have evolved and have captured significant audiences of professionals within their specific interest area. These sites are characteristically very responsive, highly specialised zones that have a highly focused approach to their target audience. Publicity in such media frames is usually very focused and relevant. Whilst the message may only reach a relatively small number of readers, it is still extremely valuable if they are the people that can make the decisions.

Target Your Efforts
While an entrepreneur has a flair for creating a product and defining the market, this is more commonly achieved through wide publicity. This is where a good PR firm can help. A good PR agency, ideally with a background in your industry, will be able to help you build the right campaign where the right message gets across to the right audience. They should also have strong contacts to the editorial and advertising staff at the relevant trade media, to ensure you get maximum exposure through any press releases, and also the best value for your advertising.

Each Company Should Have its Own PR Strategy
You can often be surprised at how many opportunities media offers you to get in touch with your market segment. You may not automatically think of online media. You can also consider sending out press releases to other countries that may be open to your products or services – something that can be done at minimal cost. PR agencies can rightly argue that they add value by sharing their knowledge about the media sector, and they can guide you to choose the right PR-strategy.

Printed matter:
Printed matter for use both before and after the trade show is an important part of the marketing campaign.

Make sure that your printed matter is written to and for the customer. Focus on what the benefits are, and initially forget about revealing which properties your products and services have.

Checklist for successful printed matter:
- Focus on customer benefits
- Write concisely
- Include many illustrations – images can often say more than words
- Avoid errors – it seems frivolous and unprofessional

Avoid handing out expensive materials because the biggest part gets thrown out after the exhibition anyway. It is much more efficient to send out more information after the trade show. The first priority, however, is to try to book a meeting. Printed matter does not sell by itself; people do.

Printed matter must be creative! Here are two examples from Alvin Therkelsen (Therkel-grafisk.dk)

1.
CEBRA PROFIL wanted to give their customers and prospects a commercial gimmick with a reminder effect, and they also wanted to issue a larger catalogue and briefly inform about the company.

Merely issuing the catalogue was very costly in postage.

In order to cut down on the costs of postage and printing, we designed a profile brochure that included the gimmick.

The gimmick was a USB memory stick that had the CEBRA PROFIL company logo printed on it. This branded the company every time the memory stick was used. Simultaneously, the catalogue was placed on the memory stick so the customers could access the catalogue directly from their computer.

As an extra "bonus", a small competition was also placed on the memory stick. This meant that a very high number of recipients viewed the contents of the memory stick, participated in the competition, saw the catalogue, read about CEBRA PROFIL and were reminded of the company every time they used the memory stick.

2.
The competition in the cleaning industry is very tough.

FBT Rengøring, a Danish cleaning company, had a reasonable market share, but they wanted to get in touch with – and meet – 100 very specific people in large companies so they could share information about their core services.

The Danish graphics design company, Therkel Grafisk, developed the following idea:
A broom without a shaft was sent out to each and every one of the 100 prospects. On the broom itself was a label simply stating "Call Christine – and we will bring the shaft".

At the same time there was a poster in the tube that provided information regarding the services the cleaning company could provide.

So, by calling Christine, the customer could get the other half of their free gift but, more importantly, Christine could get a meeting with the prospective customer.

The response was excellent! The recipients liked the idea which was innovative and funny, and they would were happy to have a meeting – and get the shaft to the broom.

Chapter 2: Planning

In the planning phase there are quite a few questions that need answering:

- How do trade shows fit into your marketing strategy?
- Why do you attend trade shows?
- What are you putting on display?
- Who are the decision-makers in your target group?
- What is your budget?

There are many reasons why companies exhibit at trade shows. E.g.:

1. Selling to visitors
2. Selling to other exhibitors
3. Getting sales leads for their sales force
4. Networking with others in the same industry
5. Creating a market brand
6. Meeting existing customers
7. Meeting customers who are otherwise difficult to arrange meetings with
8. Introducing new products
9. Marketing research
10. Finding new distributors and partners
11. Finding new employees

12. Getting press coverage

The ultimate goal of most companies is to sell their services / products.

To get an idea of what it takes to make a sale, here is a formula for how you can get up to 28 sales out of 900 contacts:

Profit formula:

Number of sales = number of meetings x (% of closed sales orders).
Number of meetings = contacts x (% of booked meetings).
Number of contacts = sales leads x (% of share in target group).
Sales leads = number of contacted guests at trade show.
Number of contacted guests at show = time x staff.

3 members of staff are at the stand for 20 hours. Every employee contacts 15 guests at the trade show per hour: 60 hours x 15 persons = 900 contacts.

We assume that, out of 900 contacted trade show guests, 25 % are in the target group = 225 contacts that potentially can be booked for a meeting.
A meeting will be arranged with approx. 25% of the contacts; approx. 56 client meetings.
A sale will be closed approx. 50% of the time = 28 sales.

When we know a bit about these figures, it is easier to make a budget for the trade show.

What does your % look like? Make a calculation of your expected sales.

In order to find out whether or not it can pay off to attend the trade show, the company has to do a Marketing RETURN ON INVESTMENT (ROI), where all known marketing efforts are accounted for: Number of hot sales leads and number of sales by each media in relation to expenditure.

Put the results into a table, so it is easier to see what yields the highest number of hot sales leads and what results in the highest number of sales.

In this context, a pre-trade show marketing campaign and a post-trade show campaign must be included in the price of trade show leads.

Media	Price per lead	Number of hot sales leads received	Price per sales lead	Closed Sales per sales lead

The budget for the trade show should include the following:

- Rental of stand
- Stand expenses: construction, carpet, lighting, etc.
- Freight and travel costs
- Staff costs
- Marketing
- Follow-up

Planning Your Tasks - Checklist

9 Months in Advance:
Evaluate the relevant trade shows. Choose where to place your stand and pay the deposit. Start planning the trade show. Choose the employees you want to participate.
Define the budget for the trade show Book accommodation, if necessary.
Stand material is purchased or retrieved – and checked.
Potential banners and graphics ordered from the graphic designers.

6 Months in Advance:
Marketing department – external / internal – to get started with printed materials and campaigns.
Copywriter gets started on press releases.
Consider a trade show training course for your participating staff.

3 Months in Advance:
Place orders for food, electricity, data, etc.
Conduct trade show training of staff. This needs to happen right before the show. 3 months before and they'll have forgotten
Launch pre-trade show marketing activities.

During the planning period, it is important to find out what is needed so your booth stands out from the rest. If possible, you can conduct brainstorming sessions with your staff so you can get a couple of creative ideas to work with:

Should there be gifts and competitions?
How do you get business cards from guests?
How do you qualify the guests, i.e. what questions do you ask for clarifying whether or not they are relevant for you? Consider making a chart recording the guests that are relevant sales leads.
It is important to make it easy to follow up on the sales leads from the trade shows. Therefore, there must be room for the following on the chart:

- Company name – all contact information
- Guest name
- Interests of the sales lead (which products)
- Decision-making competence
- Field where you can fill in next contact
- Field for samples / brochure that will be forwarded
- Comment field
- Scale from 1 - 5: How hot is this sales lead?

If you are yet to meet the relevant company's contact person, it would be a good idea to ask who the right contact is, and subsequently phone the person in question after the trade show. Here is a good approach to the subject:

"I met your colleague _____ at trade show _____.

He told me to contact you regarding a meeting about
_____."

This could make it substantially easier to get in touch with the company and arrange a meeting.

Building the Stand

When you build the trade show stand, it is important to create an open and simple décor that is both colourful and inviting.

Do not pack the stand. It will appear messy and unstructured.

Make sure that there are no counters or other barriers between guests and staff.

An example of a simple and open stand from a Danish wine dispenser company

Flowers / plants liven up your stand, and chairs for the customers may prove a hit, especially come the end of the day.

Think about visual attraction! – If possible, you can use a computer screen with a presentation or film to get the attention of passing visitors.

Ensure that the communication regarding your services / products and prices is clear.

Place the products that you would like people to see, study and talk about, at elbow and eye level. Also place them close to where people walk by. Generally, a lot of exhibitors place their products on a table which is often too low and too easy to overlook.

Remember to put yourself in the place of the visitors – what would attract you?

Think of the stand as an exhibition that is simple, welcoming, and, at the same time, attracts attention. You could take a look at museums and art exhibitions, where the displayed items struggle to get significant attention from visitors.
A good idea is to find a museum exhibit that, more than any others, attracts your attention. Try to figure out what makes the difference.

It may be a good idea to create a theme for the exhibition because it can create a good deal of attention. However, it has to fit in with the presented products – otherwise it may seem too frivolous.

Pay attention to the following points when you construct your stand:

- Visual
- Auditory
- Olfactory (e.g. the smell of freshly baked bread)
- Gustatory (e.g. samples of food)
- Sensory

Visual
It takes a guest 6 seconds to walk past your stand. That means you have 6 seconds to draw their attention, tell your story and express the benefits you have to offer.
That is why the graphical expression of your stand must be attractive and selling.
Test your signposting on several individuals that are not connected to the company, before you decide on what you want to use at the trade show.

Auditory
What can you implement in order to make your stand more efficient? Music, sound effects or a microphone placed on a salesman that presents the product.

Olfactory
Should you place a popcorn maker, flowers or a professional scent machine somewhere in the stand?
Today we have companies that specialize in creating scents that make us think and react in certain ways.

Gustatory
Is it possible to sample your product? Or can you give a delicious tasting experience during a short exhibition talk? This could have a very positive impact.

Sensory
Some people are most comfortable when they can feel the product in question. Therefore it is always a good idea to allow your guests to try out and hold the product, if the opportunity arises.

Handouts:
There are several things you should take into consideration regarding the material you hand out at the trade show.
You may lose the customer if he is unable to find what he is looking for in the material. Needless to say, things may also go wrong if you do not have any material at all.
It might be better to send him the info after the show. If he takes it with him it goes in the plastic bag with piles of literature from everybody else and probably never comes out to be looked at! If it lands on his desk it stands out!
Also, if he can take it with him he is less likely to give you his contact details.
Always remember that the very best thing is a personal meeting after the trade show. Here you have an opportunity to sell, create a need and to enthuse.

The shrewdest thing to do is to produce material that is only intended for the trade show. If it is possible to produce the material conjointly with a business partner at the show, which could refer to your booth number, it may prove beneficial for both parties.

Some kind of competition could also attract visitors: A draw, perhaps, on the basis of the visitors who put their business cards in a bowl at the stand.

When you receive a business card, you could write down a little something about the person for later use in your follow-up form.

Chapter 3: At the Exhibition

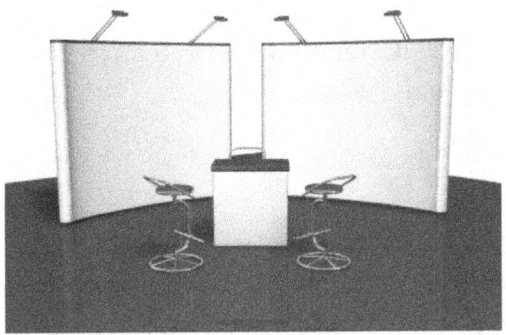

General advice on good sales behaviour:
- Be genuinely interested in other people.
- Smile, smile, smile.
- Remember that a man's /woman's name is the nicest and most important sound in any language.
- Be a good listener.
- Encourage the other person to talk about himself/herself.
- Talk about the other person's interests.
- Make sure that the other person feels important – and do it sincerely.
- Avoid engaging in heated arguments.
- Respect the other person's opinions.
- Commence with a question that the other person will have to answer with a yes or, alternatively, an open question.
- Allow the other person to speak.
- Try to honestly see things from the other person's point of view.
- Sympathise with the other person and his/her situation.
- Describe the benefits of your product / service with pictures and examples. Use any kind of storytelling – create a story about the product / service. Focus

on SPECIFIC benefits that you have identified from your discussions

At trade shows you have to take the time factor into account when thinking about the advice given above. Preferably, you have to reach a number of 15 contacts per hour unless, of course, you are dealing with a very hot sales lead. In these cases it is always better to spend an hour with a true lead than 4 minutes each with 15 time wasters.

When dealing with a very hot prospect, you use the necessary amount of time and, if possible, aim directly towards closing the sale.

When you have visitors in your stand, it is important to know about distances between people – physically as well as mentally and emotionally:

Most people are familiar with phrases such as:

- "Too close for comfort"
- "A clingy person"
- "She's invading my personal space"

It is well known that both animals and humans demonstrate territorial behaviour in order to mark their boundaries.

Social zone: (Distance: 1.30 m – 2.25 m)

An example is the distance between people at a social gathering at their workplace.

Personal zone: (Distance: 80 cm – 1.30 m) Similar to what we call keeping a person "at an arm's length".

Close distance: (Distance: 50 cm – 80 cm) Here you can actually grab a hold of the person.
Intimate zone: (Distance: 15 cm – 50 cm) If people are pushed together during rush hour on a train or in an elevator, you can avoid contact by staying totally motionless and, at the same time, fixate your eyes on the floor indicator. The intimate zone can be characterised as the erotic, comfort and protective zone.

Active Listening
When you have visitors in your stand make them feel welcome by using active listening.

To listen actively:
If you want to improve your active listening skills, you must have a genuine respect for the recipient's personal values and integrity.

This implies that you have to respect the thoughts and feelings that others may have, even though you fundamentally disagree.

In the role as the 'active' listener, you have to proceed actively and dynamically in order to understand the content of what is being said.
You have to be as neutral as possible, don't judge, criticise or moralise.

DO NOT interrupt. Give the visitor the opportunity to finish talking. It can be especially important to get things said in the beginning of a conversation.

Do not stress the person that is talking. Do not look at your watch, and do not drum your fingers on the table. Do not hush people.

What are your considerations when you want a constructive dialog with another person?

It is primarily the spoken language that creates a trustworthy environment and should, subsequently, lead to a mutual understanding.

Tone of voice and intonation help express a person's commitment, and the understanding of what is being said is largely depending on this.

Body language is used to support what is being said, and it may even have a greater influence on the person you are talking to than the words and their meaning.

How do you use your voice?

Do you speak in a low, loud or monotonous voice, or do you adjust the vocal strength to the situation at hand? Do you change the pace appropriately along the way? Do you speak with empathy and commitment?

How do you use your body?

Do you always seek eye contact, or does this depend on the person you are talking to?

Do you use gestures?

Is your face calm or vivacious?

Do you move your hands when talking?

Are your hands calm or so tightly clenched that your knuckles almost turn white?

Do you have a straight and open posture?

Or is your posture drooping, stooping and closed?

Listening – obstacles

A human being is equipped with two ears and only one mouth because we have to listen twice as much as we speak. This can be incredibly difficult because we are so eager to tell our customers about everything we have to offer.

Therefore, the very first obstacle we encounter is ourselves. We have to concentrate 100% on listening.

The reason is that there are a lot of other obstacles that also need to be taken into account. These are often obstacles we are unable to remedy. Instead we need to accept them and work under the given conditions.

You have to be aware if the obstacle lies with you or your potential customer.

Here are some examples of listening obstacles you can come across at a trade show:

- Physical condition
- Hearing-impairment

- Fatigue / hunger or thirst
- State of mind / emotions / personal interests
- Personal attitudes
- Preconceived ideas
- Prejudice
- Reaction to the narrator's behaviour, appearance, voice, accent, dialect, etc.
- Influence of ambient noise / obstruction of view
- Interruptions

The 4x20 Rule

There is a lot of nonverbal communication when two people meet for the first time:

The initial 20 seconds (time)
The initial 20 cm (face)
The initial 20 words (speech)
The initial 20 paces (movement)

Always remember, when meeting another person, you will be assessed on:

- An exciting opening line
- Your interest in the customer
- Clothing
- Level of grooming
- Level of understanding of customer's situation
- Speaking at a reasonable speed
- Enthusiasm and an open body language
- Displaying an honest interest in the customer
- Listening to the customer – also with your eyes
- Demonstrating commitment to your work
- Eye contact

- A genuine smile
- Praising the customer
- Being happy and positive

You should have a plan regarding the 4x20 rule for what you do when you are at the trade show.

What do you do in the initial 20 seconds?
How about your face – are you smiling or do you have wrinkles on your forehead?
How do you move – do you stand up straight or do you literally look like you have been hung out to dry?

What do you say when a trade show guest walks past your stand?
How do you get guests to visit your stand? Many people make the classic mistake of asking if there is anything they can help with.

Examples of good opening lines could be:

"What brings you to the trade show today?"
"What company do you represent?"
"Step inside the stand."
"Hi, my name is _____ (reach out your hand)."

Here are some examples of good sales questions you can ask at your stand:

1. What is your purpose with visiting the trade show?
2. What is your strategy for the future?
3. Who is your current provider?

4. What do you like about it the most (your product)?
5. If you could have it exactly the way you wanted it, what would you change?
6. What could make you replace your current provider?
7. What is your experience with _____?
8. Is there anything else you'd like to see?
9. Have you considered any alternatives?
10. Do you have any questions?
11. What is your/the next step?
12. Is there anyone but yourself help make the decision?
13. Do you have a deadline?
14. When would you like to start?
15. When shall we meet again?
16. When do you wish to receive your delivery?

Observe body language:

Body language is the postures, gestures and facial expressions that, along with pauses, accents and other nonverbal signals, accompany words in the conversation.

The body language is especially interesting because it expresses our current state of mind, including our sympathy and empathy towards the person we are talking to.
Our body language also expresses our attitude, whether it is regarding the person, the subject or the situation.

When you wish to grasp the meaning of a message, you must not simply listen to the words, but also the body language.

Time and again you can experience discrepancy between spoken words and body signals.
In these cases you can proceed as active listeners and ask inquisitively until you experience concordance.

Body language is culturally determined. This means that the same signals easily can have different meanings in different cultures.

First Impression

You only have one chance of making a good first impression. It is good to start a conversation with an exciting opening line that shows an interest in your customer's business, or the customer himself.

Assignment:

Create your own examples of good opening lines:

_____

_____

_____

_____

_____

_____

It is important that your attire matches the target audience you expect to see at your stand.

Be well-dressed at all times. It is better to seem overdressed than sloppy. Your standards of hygiene must be high and you have to be well groomed.

Brush your teeth – do not smell of garlic. Always keep a breath mint or mouth spray in your pocket. Use a type of deodorant / aftershave that is not too heavy, strong-scented or dominant.

You must be mentally prepared when you show up at the exhibition.

It is important to have a positive attitude. Tell yourself:

- Today's going to be a good day

- We can make today great
- We will put a smile on the face of our customers
- Our goal will be easy to achieve
- We are the best
- We make a difference
- We have a great product

Rapport – Wavelength

We prefer doing business with people like ourselves. That is why it is important to get on the same wavelength.
It is easier to get on the same wavelength with people we have something in common with. Try to find a common frame of reference as quickly as possible, and then try to find out more and more things you have in common with the customer.

You can adjust and customize your manner of speaking, intonation and body language so it matches the customer.

It is important to maintain an enthusiastic and open body language during the entire process.

It is also very important that you listen to the customers. Look them in the eye when necessary. Take notes and nod. Feel free to smile when it is appropriate.

If you can use humour, and even get the customer to laugh with you, it is an incredibly good sign. It is also a clear signal that you are dealing with an open-minded client.

It is important that you do not criticise your competitors during a presentation – respect them.
You can, of course, highlight what you are good at, but never claim that the competitors are inferior.
A very common question is why you are better than the competitors. Here you have to tread carefully and maybe refrain from saying the things you are most eager to say. Instead focus on not being critical.

Potential response:
"Our competitors are good at what they do, but some of the things we hear from our customers, is that we especially distinguish ourselves with regards to our
_____ (USP).
Tell me what you pay special attention to?"

Possible response:
"I am no expert on our competitors; other people in our company know more about that than I do. I focus on how our clients can gain the most from what we have to offer. Tell me, were you thinking about something specific?"

Analyse Customer Needs
Ask about the customer's needs with open questions.
Get the customer to experience his needs so strongly that he has to get his needs met.
Do not introduce the customer to the solution before he strongly experiences the need for it.

Enthusiasm! – And a Firm Belief in Your Product
The customer will be more convinced by your enthusiasm than by your way of explaining the usage.
That is why it is important that you maintain your enthusiasm throughout the day. Also when you have had many presentations, and they possibly have not gone as well as you could have hoped for. I would even go as far as saying that sales are spread across 80% enthusiasm and 20% product knowledge.

I can help you along the way, but ultimately you must show that you are able to place yourself in the customer's situation.

It is important that you try to seek out all the relevant information about the customer that you possibly can during the short stretch of time that is available at the trade show:

- Current and future needs
- Company history
- Number of branches
- Number of employees
- Products
- Revenue
- Contact persons
- News
- Expansions
- Other specialities, etc...

You can use all of this information in the conversation with the customer. It helps you adapt your presentation to your customer's needs.

When you are talking to the right contact, it is important that you are able to properly sell yourself and establish what chances you have of making a sale in the short or in the long run. You must also consider the following things:

• Smile with your voice. Speak loud and clear. Be 100% certain of what you are going to say.

• For you to obtain a "yes" when in a deal situation, trying to book an appointment or trying to procure time for a follow-up sales conversation, your customer has to feel that his time will be well invested. Your product can provide savings and / or increased market or revenue opportunities. In other words, the customer needs to be aware of all the potential benefits.

The conclusion of your conversation aims at stimulating customer interest in your product and making him so curious that he will be dying to get more detailed information, to buy, or to make an appointment.

It is essential that you do not drag out the end of the conversation for too long, and that you are able to direct the visitor towards checking his diary. E.g.:

• "What does your calendar look like in, say, week xx or yy?"
• "What is most suitable for you – Monday or Tuesday?"
• "What is most suitable for you – xxxday at xx a.m. / p.m. or xx a.m. / p.m.?"

This is, of course, assuming that your goal is to arrange a meeting where you subsequently can make a sale.

If the goal is to sell right here and right now, the time has come to carry out a test close.

Test Close
Every time you see or hear a signal to buy, you ask a test closing question. E.g. you can ask:

"With regards to the things we've been looking at just now, what does it sound / look like to you?"
-or
"If we try to figure something out…" This is called a test close.

Here are three examples of test closings:

• "Based on what we have been looking at up to now, what does it look like? – sound like? – feel like?"
• "If you choose to try out our product, when do you want it delivered?"
• "How do you think your (boss/co-worker/wife/husband) would like it?"

By asking one of the questions above, you can get a picture of how close / far you are from closing a sale. Depending on the visitor's response, there are basically just three options you can pursue:

1. Ask for the order
2. Make a new and rephrased test close
3. Continue to sell

It is all about narrowing the test closes in to such an extent, and in a natural way, where you make the visitor talk himself into placing an order. Depending on the visitor response, it can be necessary to come up with more product features and advantages / benefits, eventually magnifying the visitor's product need to such an extent that he places an order or arranges a meeting or any other kind of follow-up arrangement.

It is usually the case that we are all controlled by 2 factors: **pleasure** or the **fear of pain or discomfort**. In order to really create a need or desire for a product, it is usually a good idea that one of the product characteristics or benefits provides **pleasure**. It may, for example, be in the form of increased productivity, higher profits, happier employees or anything else that gives the visitor pleasure, savings or dividends.
The second factor is **fear**. You can use this factor to convince the visitor that your product / service and solution can consolidate the client's position on the market, prevent accidents or keep your employees from turning sulky or even changing jobs.

It is always easier to find arguments that go in the direction of pleasure, but it can definitely be worth it to sit down and find some arguments that play on fear (fear of loss).

When can you test close a sale? The answer is: **ALWAYS**! You can always test close. A test close is to get the visitor's opinion on the thing that you are presenting to him. Test closes can be used when you sense or hear a buying signal from the visitor (when the guest expresses a change of attitude or indicates that he is well-disposed towards your offer).

You can complete a test close by asking for the visitor's opinion or putting the small word "if" in front of a closed question that reveals the visitor's opinion.

"If" is the ultimate word when it comes to test closes:

- "If we are to co-operate, when do we start?"
- "If we reach an agreement, when do you want delivery?"

Presentation Techniques at the Trade Show
Present how your product or service can create profits / value for the visitor – relate it to what you have been talking about.
You probably have a lot of excellent reasons why the visitor should buy *your* product. However, only a few are likely to be the *main* reasons. Present the most important benefits that the visitor emphasises.
It is also important that you know how your product / services directly benefit the customer.
A PAG-table is used as a model to uncover the properties, possible advantages and potential benefits of the products or services that you represent.

Fill out the PAG-table on one feature of your product or service, see how many "possible advantages" you can find and what benefits each of these will give your customers.

Properties (Is)
Possible advantages (Does)
Potential gain (Significance)

Properties:	Advantages:	Gains:

Describe the **properties** of the product.
A property is fact, typically something that can be seen, felt or measured. E.g. service, service inspection, consulting, delivery time, etc...
Describe how the individual characteristics of your product or service will be of **advantage** to your customer. A single property can typically produce several possible advantages.
Tangibly describe the customer **gains**. In this context it could mean: money saved, time saved, etc.

The PAG-model is a good tool helping you argue effectively in favour of your product / service. The strength of this model is that it originates from within the properties of your product. The trick now is to convert these properties into advantages, and eventually focus on the gains the customer will receive when purchasing your suggested solution.

There are many advantages in drawing up a PAG-model. These include:

• Increased product knowledge
• Amplifying your ability to ask the "right" questions in order to check whether the possible advantages of your product / service also supply your customer with a potential gain.

One of the main advantages of the PAG-model is that it allocates more peace to work during the sales conversation. The basis is that you will become much better at linking your customer assessments with plausible advantages.

This allows you to reinforce your argumentation when dealing with the customer because you know exactly what potential benefits you are arguing in favour of. If you are unable to use advantages and gains when arguing in favour of a property, this property has no value.

Product properties (Is)
Possible advantages (Does)
Potential gains (Significance)

Share your product or service gains in a way that make a real difference for the trade show guest.

Position what you sell as being at the right price compared to the gains the customer will receive.

During sales a potential customer will always make a balancing of price compared to gains - something like a pharmacist's scales.

Gains   Price

If the gains outweigh the cost, the customer will make the purchase.

Convince the guest that the time is right to buy.
If you have analyses, or any other types of evidence that may substantiate the gains of your product, be sure to implement these in your presentation – preferably with visual graphs.

Examples or stories from people, who have benefited greatly from your product, are also very convincing during a presentation.
It can prove very efficient if you are able to demonstrate your product on the spot. However, it may prove to be an even better idea if you demonstrate the product during a meeting where you also have the opportunity of closing the deal right away.

Sometimes, when you try to sell something, e.g. a bouquet, it looks much better when you wrap it in cellophane. When you describe your product, it is always good to wrap it in what I call "cellophane words". Thus, the value of your product is likely to increase if you wrap it in cellophane words.

Cellophane Words:
Trust
Empathy
Safety
Security
Guarantee
Time
Stability
Savings
Unique
Exclusive
Advantage
Benefit
Durable
Maintenance-free
Advantageous
Attractive
Valuable
Achieve
Benign
Opportunity
Value
Revenue
Enjoy
Progress
Beneficial
Future-proof
Pleasure

Desirable
Exceptional
Lovely
Gain
Maximising
Cost reductions (time, money, resources, etc.)

Your trade show presentation must be a so-called elevator pitch. The length of the pitch should be kept under 60 seconds. Therefore, it is important that you are able to explain, in an appealing way, what you can help with – especially if you are in the service industry.

The elevator pitch should include:
1. Who you are and who you can help (who are your customers / clients)
2. What you can help with – i.e. the results you / your clients will get from working with you. Do not fall into the old trap of talking about properties.
3. The value / gains you can give your customers / clients. Appeal to emotions and sense of logic.

When you prepare a longer presentation, it is important that you have an "objection bank" containing answers to objections and questions you might expect from customers.

Chapter 4: Manning / Staff

Without a dynamic staff at the trade show, all of your marketing activities, eye-catching displays and signposting can be a waste of money. The staff on your stand are the lifeblood of your trade show strategy.

Your employees represent your company during the trade show. They personify the quality and image of your product. They are responsible for prequalifying your visitors as well as establishing relations and themes to be used in the follow- up after the trade show.

In other words, the effectiveness of your exhibition team is crucial for your success at any trade show. For this reason, your stand staff should be the ablest and smartest representatives from your organisation: Those who are really enthusiastic about your product, those who are the best communicators and sellers, those who provide exceptional customer service.

If you need volunteers they need a comprehensive training in all aspects of your organisation:

- Products
- Trade show goal
- Target group
- USP
- Sales pitch/script

Tell the trade show staff what is expected of them. This includes how to dress, and how long they will have to be on the stand. They must show etiquette (i.e. abstain from eating, drinking or sitting down). Above all, they have to be courteous and professional.

Do not overcrowd your stall with staff in such a way that visitors do not dare to enter.

In case visitors are sparse, it is very important to keep your spirits up because your face and charisma sell. A sulky and disillusioned salesman is not particularly inviting.

When you return from the trade show, be sure to follow up immediately with phone calls or personal letters and invitations to meetings where you will discuss the next step.

If you do not have the time for the follow-up yourself, it is a good idea to use a telemarketing agency.

A trade show could be a good opportunity to do some team building, both before and after the show, because the staff members are going to work closely with one another while being away from home and the structure of their everyday surroundings.

At the same time, a trade show is a welcome opportunity to refresh sales training.

Classical Errors to Avoid:

1. Too much telling, too little selling
2. Talking too much, perhaps using too many technical terms not understood by all
3. Focusing on telling about properties instead of telling the customer what he wants to hear, namely the gains
4. Spending too much time on individual visitors
5. Not actively pursuing the order, the meeting or the next step

The challenging differences between ordinary sales and trade show sales are:

- Both buyer and seller are displaced from their familiar surroundings
- Many distractions
- It can be difficult to get your information out there through all the exhibitors / competitors who sell the same thing as you
- The visitors may be tired from walking around the trade show all day

Physical Preparation of Staff:
Normally we quickly forget how strenuous it is to stand on a concrete floor and be friendly to visitors all day.
That is why it is important that your trade show employees are in a good physical shape. This ensures a high level of energy.

It is actually a good idea to warm up and stretch before you get on with your day. It is also a good idea to incorporate breaks where your staff can stretch their legs and move around the place a bit.

Food and Drink
Healthy food, without too much salt, is the best before, during and after the trade show. Get a good, hearty breakfast, and be sure to have plenty of fresh fruit and plenty of mineral water at the stand.
Restrict or ban alcohol before and during the trade show. Avoid anything that can cause bad breath.

Attire
Here are a few examples of trade show clothing:

1. Suit, shirt and tie.
You can place your company logo on the chest or collar of the shirt. You can also order ties with your logo printed, embroidered or woven on it.

2. Jeans, polo / t-shirt and soft shell jacket.
Logo can be placed on the back and chest of all three tops.

3. Canvas trousers, polo shirt and cardigan.
You can place the company logo on the polo's back and chest as well as on the chest of the cardigan.

You just have to figure out if you want to signal business, active employees or casual style.

It is my personal opinion that some kind of trade show uniform, matching the products being sold, is the best solution.

Pay special attention to good shoes.

Attach your name tag to your chest on the top right hand side. That makes it more noticeable for the people you greet.

The Worst Errors:

1. Ignoring customers (internal chatter)
2. Not knowing the products well enough
3. Eating at the stand
4. Interrupting
5. Hands firmly placed in your pocket
6. Trying to keep the visitors in your stand, even though it is evident that they want to move on
7. Too much contact / too close for comfort
8. Chewing gum
9. Clearing your throat too loudly
10. Bad breath

Ready for Action

Always make the front of your stand face the corridor where people walk by. It may become necessary to go out into the corridor and talk to people, if visits to your stand are scarce. This is a difficult challenge that must be prepared for, using script and role-playing, in order to make it work.

- Body language and mental attitude must be ready.

- Smile and make eye contact. Give a firm handshake.

- Find the opening line that suits your company:

For the active visitors:
- "Thank you for visiting our stand. What caught your attention?"
- "I can tell that you're interested in xxxxx. Are you familiar with our product?"
- "It looks like you are familiar with our company. Are you looking for something specific?"

Uncertain / expressionless visitors:
- "What did you want to see at the trade show?"
- "Are you looking for something in particular?"
- "What is the most exciting part of the trade show?"
- "Did anything at the trade show interest you?"

This is How You Influence a Trade Show Visitor:

Place yourself in a position where the visitor can see into your stand. Make sure that there are as few distractions as possible.

Use your body language to lead visitors into your stand, even using oral invitations if necessary.

Qualify

Be professionally inquisitive and ask questions like: "What kind of work do you perform in your company?" Ask about potential areas of responsibility.

Identify if you can help / sell anything to the company. If that is not the case, nicely bid farewell so you can focus on the next visitor as quickly as possible.

What Should a Visitor Receive from You?
- Contact name
- Business card
- One elevator pitch at the very least
- A plan for what to do next

Schedule
Make a form with visitor information. Make sure you have a stapler so you can attach your business card to the form.

Chapter 5: Tips, Tricks and Secrets

A client recently told me: "Our business has been going so well in the last five years that we haven't felt the need to do anything about sales training. Things are different now – we need help!"

In today's market, experiencing a financial crisis of epic proportions, there is an intense competition for customers.

When a salesman is unprepared for cold calling, and the market is not ready to buy, trade shows are a good place to get into contact with potential customers.

In a tough market, an untrained salesman will reply to a price objection in the following way: "Well, let me see what I can do." Is it really all about the price, or is it about the value and gains? Let us contemplate a couple of solutions you can implement to differentiate yourself from your competitors.

What is the value?

The truth is that value, like beauty, is subjective. It is all about the eye of the beholder.

It rests in the hands of every professional salesman to find out exactly how to create value for customers. Be sure to listen and ask the questions that raise awareness of the value / gains of your product or service.

Learn how to sell gains and how to differentiate yourselves from your competitors.

Use a PAG-table to highlight the gains for yourself. (The PAG-table is described in Chapter 3).

Your potential customers may be eager to compare your solution with other solutions. The main point here is: If you cannot create a strong and distinct difference for the customer, it will look as if everyone carries the same product or service. So, the question is: How can you distinguish yourself and your offer from the competition?

Here are a few options:

Product Differentiation

Focus on how your product or service is different or better than what your competitors have to offer. If you are unable to come up with some unique differences, you risk being perceived as just another basic commodity.

Price Differentiation

A great deal of marketing is based on the fact that the best way to sell is undercut everyone else. Narrow margins have run more companies out of business than any other single factor.

By having multiple qualities and multiple options, price differentiation can make negotiation easier. We know from negotiation techniques that negotiating becomes easier when we include several parameters. It is also a good idea to cut the sales commission on the cheapest products, thereby motivating your sales staff to sell more of your expensive products or services, thus increasing their commission.

Relations Create Results

Build a relationship based on a high level of trust between you and your customers. Building a firm trust, with a high level of integrity, is a win-win strategy. Always give the customer something that exceeds his expectations. Be prepared to win customer trust. It takes time, requires planning and persistency, but it makes a world of difference on your bottom line.

Examine Your Business Processes

Many companies are still guided by ancient business models: "We've never done it that way"-syndrome. The syndrome bites us in the backside when we neglect to implement innovative ideas into our business methods. Get your best minds to work together – brainstorm what could create better and more customer-friendly out-of-the-box ways of doing business.

Always remember that the business community changes each and every day because of globalisation, e-commerce, internet and new software programs.

Take advantage of innovation instead of becoming a victim of it!

Technological Differentiation

Modern technology gives us many opportunities of promoting our ways of serving customers and communicating with them more efficiently. The new forms of communication include a wide variety of options:

- Podcasts that keep customers up-to-date
- A blog that gives you the opportunity to "hear" from your clients

- Video conferencing with clients, both internally and externally
- Online live chat on websites
- SMS solutions
- Mobile websites

Always remember: Make it easy for your customers to communicate with you and buy from you.

Reference Sales

Can you provide your customers with outstanding customer service and extraordinary experiences, so they start telling their friends and colleagues about you?
A customer miracle is when a customer says "Wow!" Ask yourselves: "How can we transform the act of doing business with us into an irresistible experience?" If your sales process is so convincing that your sales leads see you, and what you offer, as irresistible, it makes your competitors irrelevant!

Remember that people are always willing to pay for expertise, and they prefer doing business with people they know and trust.

More Tips

If you can convince a well-known personality to visit your stand, it may prove a major attraction. This must then be printed on the invitations so the yield is maximised.

A gift in 2 parts can also ensure that the right people show up. E.g. they can receive a gift at the trade show and subsequently receive the other half during a follow-up meeting.

Send a map marking your stand at the trade show, along with other practical information.

Make an ice cream cone sign with a selling or interesting headline that gets the audience to pause for a while. Think: Gain, gain, gain!

Make video recordings of trade show visitors commenting on your product at the stand. It is always interesting to see what is being filmed. If you there is enough space, then you can make a small study with a background.
It is a huge advantage if a customer speaks favourably about your product. This makes it much easier to sell the product afterwards. Who knows, maybe some of the statements are good enough to be used in future marketing campaigns.

If it is possible to make raffles, and you announce the draw at the show, it is a clever way of getting some exposure to your company name. And, if you have ongoing raffles, this can cause more traffic to and from your stand. Think of it as complimentary radio advertising for qualified visitors.

Use your senses – and be remembered

By violinist Karen Humle – www.violinconsult.com

Try to compare a trade show experience with a piece of music.

It would be what you call a cacophony in the musical jargon, i.e. a chaotic jumble of different expressions. How do you ensure that both you and the things you present at the trade show are remembered subsequently?

A very important thing that makes people remember you is talking directly to their emotions and senses when they experience you and your product.

Artistic expressions are great when creating experiences on an emotional level. We experience things quite differently when they are conveyed to us through music, pictures or play-acting.

In my capacity as a professional violinist I have created a concept in my consulting company, Violinconsult, where I convert words and moods into musical expressions. This opens up the opportunity of working with development on a completely different emotional level. At a trade show, sensory experiences, combined with your product, will leave the recipient with a lasting impression.

So give people an experience, but not only as an entertaining gimmick.
Use your product as a starting point, and let the value and content of your product form the basis of a true experience for the recipient.

If you sell a physical product, you could pay an artist to decorate a few unique specimens during the trade show. These specimens could then become prizes in your competition.

You could also hire a couple of actors to illustrate the excellent service your company provides, preferably using some products from your company as props.

A musical piece, created specifically for your concept or brand, performed live at the trade show.

A dancer, who, combined with your product's target audience, transforms the strengths and precision of your product into a small ballet or hip hop routine.

A couple of short performances along the way will create visibility and interest in your stand and your product. However, it has to be authentic and take its starting point in the products or services you provide.

The possibilities are endless, and I do not think we can even begin to grasp the boundaries on the countless levels of expressing values.

Chapter 6: Follow-up

Most companies probably gain the most during the follow-up.
It is often the case that sales people cannot find the time to follow up on all the relevant leads they get at trade shows. This is a very annoying tendency and a real shame because trade show leads are considerably better than normal leads.

Visitors at trade shows are better buyers, among other things, because they are willing to *attend* the trade show. They are likely to know what they want, so your task is to deliver it to them.

You will get the chance to look people in the eye at the trade show, and possibly even gain their trust. This is a great advantage compared to your competitors who have to start from scratch.

Trade show leads are likely to have an interest in what you have to sell in advance; otherwise they would not pay your stand a visit.

Leads at trade shows are more likely to be looking for a purchase than cold leads.

What to Do With All the Leads You Get?
What range of activities should you set in motion?
Follow-up over the telephone, newsletters, book meetings, trade show material?

Try to calculate the total price for the trade show participation, and divide it by the number of qualified leads. This gives you a price per lead.
Prices typically range from £20 - £200.
A great number of companies choose to economise on the materials they send out to very expensive leads.

If you want to make an impression, you can always send out the materials using FedEx, UPS etc., e.g. wrapping the materials in huge boxes.

Studies from the Massachusetts Center for Marketing Communications show that up to 43% of potential buyers did not receive trade show materials until after deciding to buy from another supplier. 18% never received the materials they had been promised at the trade show.

If the sales lead forms are not filled out correctly or adequately, this can be a contributing factor to why sales people are unable to follow up on potential leads. Remember to indicate how hot you believe the individual lead to be – possibly by including a scale from 0 – 5.

If your team experiences too many poor quality leads, it could mean that they do not want to continue working with them. That is why it is not always the number of leads, but also the quality of the leads that is crucial for the result.

It is crucially important to make a detailed plan for the follow-up, and also make sure you have plenty of time to deal with it when you return from the trade show:

- If sending out letters is part of the follow-up, it is important to make them as personal and as creative as possible. View examples displayed earlier in the book.
- A post-trade show gift could also be a good idea.
- Always call and make sure the customer has received the gift or letter.
- A handwritten letter of thanks is very efficient and definitely worth spending time on.
- Example: "It was interesting meeting you at the trade show, and I am looking forward to meeting you again."
- Newsletters are another way of undertaking follow-up.
- Following up over the telephone is an absolute post-trade show must.
- Questionnaire follow-up, including a prize, is also a clever way of staying in touch.
- Keep in touch with your prospects and create a strategy for follow-up.
- A prospect is a sales lead until insisting on no longer being sent more materials.
- It is very important to measure the follow-up effect on the trade show leads. Ask all your sales people to do a thorough report on the results of all leads.

What gets measured – gets done!